RISING STARS
Maths

Fluency with Fractions

TEACHER'S GUIDE

Steph King

YEAR
2

Rising Stars UK Ltd
7 Hatchers Mews, Bermondsey Street, London, SE1 3GS

www.risingstars-uk.com

Every effort has been made to trace copyright holders and obtain their permission for the use of copyright materials. The authors and publisher will gladly receive information enabling them to rectify any error or omission in subsequent editions. All facts are correct at time of going to press.

Published 2014
Reprinted 2014, 2015
Text, design and layout © Rising Stars UK Ltd.

The right of Steph King to be identified as the author of this work has been asserted by her in accordance with the Copyright, Design and Patents Act 1998.

Author: Steph King
Consultant: Cherri Moseley
Publisher: Fiona Lazenby
Project Manager: Debbie Allen
Editorial: Katharine Timberlake, Kate Manson
Cover design: Burville-Riley Partnership
Design: Marc Burville-Riley
Typesetting: Fakenham Prepress Solutions
Illustrations: Louise Forshaw / Advocate Art, Richard and Benjamin,
    Fakenham Prepress Solutions
CD-ROM development: Alex Morris

British Library Cataloguing in Publication Data.
A CIP record for this book is available from the British Library.

ISBN: 978-1-78339-181-3

Printed by: Ashford Colour Press Ltd, Gosport, Hants

MIX
Paper from
responsible sources
FSC www.fsc.org   FSC® C011748

Contents

Fractions in the 2014 National Curriculum

The National Curriculum aims to ensure that all pupils become fluent in the fundamentals of mathematics, can reason mathematically and can solve problems by applying their mathematics. With a significant shift in expectations in the 2014 Programme of Study, children are required to work with and calculate using a range of fractions at an earlier stage. Achieving fluency will depend on developing conceptual understanding through a variety of practical and contextual opportunities.

Statutory requirements and non-statutory guidance

At first glance, the statutory requirements for the Fractions domain for younger children may not appear to be that extensive. However, it is important to note that each 'objective' is made up of a range of different skills and knowledge that need to be addressed. We must remember that mastery of one aspect does not necessarily imply mastery of another.

The Programme of Study also provides non-statutory guidance that helps to clarify, secure and extend learning in each domain to best prepare children for the next stage of mathematical development. Units in this *Fluency with Fractions* series, therefore, also address some aspects of the non-statutory guidance. These objectives are flagged where applicable.

Fractions across the domains

Learning about fractions is not exclusive to the Fractions domain in the Programme of Study. Conceptual understanding of fractions is also addressed and applied through work on time, turns, angles and through many other aspects of measurement, geometry and also statistics. We must also remember to continue to practise and extend learning from previous year groups even if a concept is not explicitly covered in the Programme of Study for the current year group. The other domains provide useful opportunities for this.

Making the links: decimals, percentages, ratio and proportion

Children will first experience decimals in the context of measurement. However, security with place value is vital if they are to truly understand how the position of a digit on either side of the decimal point determines its size. Place value charts and grids are used in this series of books to continue to reinforce this concept and to help children make sense of tenths, hundredths and thousandths.

As children progress through the Programmes of Study, they will later meet percentages. Recognising that a fraction such as $\frac{25}{100}$ can be written as $25 \div 100$, and therefore as 0.25, will help make the connection to 25%.

Finding and identifying equivalent fractions will later pave the way for understanding equivalent ratios.

For this reason, within the *Fluency with Fractions* series, the Year 4 book includes work on decimals, Year 5 includes percentages and Year 6 goes on to incorporate ratio and proportion.

Developing conceptual understanding through the use of resources

Children should be given opportunities to develop conceptual understanding through a range of practical experiences and the use of visual representations to help them make sense of fractions. Manipulatives, such as Base 10 apparatus, cubes and counters, along with other resources, should be used skilfully to model concepts and provide a reference point to help children make connections for future learning. Moving in this way from concrete resources to pictorial representations to symbolic notation for fractions will help to secure conceptual understanding.

Developing mathematical language

Language is often cited as a barrier to learning, so it is important to model technical vocabulary that helps children to use it confidently and to help them explain their mathematical thinking and reasoning. Appropriate language structures are suggested throughout the Units.

Using representations to support understanding

Fractions is a part of mathematics that children often find more difficult to learn than other areas. This, in turn, is often the result of teachers finding the concepts more difficult to teach. We need to help children to see what we mean and make links to other familiar representations that they know, e.g. number lines.

Historically, images to support the teaching of fractions have tended to be related to real-life examples that children see 'cut-up' and shared. Pizzas, cakes and chocolate are examples of this. Although these representations are valuable (particularly circular images that will later inform work on pie charts), it is the linear image that directly relates to the number line that will support the transition of concrete to abstract when counting and calculating.

Throughout the *Fluency with Fractions* resources, fraction bar images are used in each year level to introduce the concept of fractions as equal parts of a whole, equivalence, counting (linked to the number line) and calculating.

The following diagrams provide a few generic examples to illustrate how different images are used. Templates for some useful images are provided on the accompanying CD-ROM.

- Fractions as equal parts of one whole.

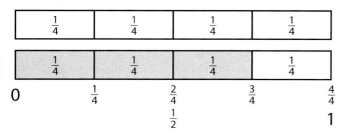

- Linking fractions to counting on a number line to reinforce that fractions are numbers in their own right. Counting paves the way for calculating.

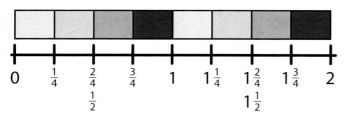

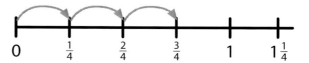

- Developing a range of images to explore equivalent fractions.

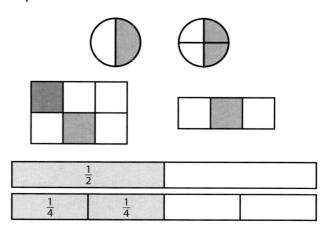

- Comparing fractions on a number line.

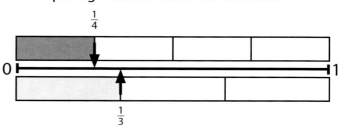

- Using fraction bars to support early calculation of fractions of amounts.

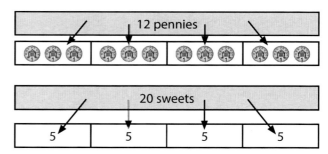

- Using fraction bars to support identifying an amount represented by a fraction.

12			

3

3	3	3	3

How to use this book

The Units in this book support the development of conceptual understanding of fractions and are intended to be used to introduce concepts. Learning should be practised and revisited regularly using other resources to consolidate and deepen understanding.

Each Unit within the books is structured in the same way, providing guidance to support teachers and an example teaching sequence.

Tasks can be used as suggested or adapted accordingly to meet the needs of each setting. Guided learning provides an opportunity for the adult to take learning forward with a group or to take part in an activity that has a greater problem-solving element and where language may be more demanding. Additional editable resource sheets are provided on the accompanying CD-ROM to support this.

Bold text shows the link to the NC objectives or the non-statutory guidance.

Please check that prior learning is in place before working on this unit.

This section helps teachers to make connections through the use of visual representations and language structures.

Each Unit includes a Talking point page that can be displayed on the interactive whiteboard or photocopied to give to children. The visual images and prompt questions help to contextualise the concept of fractions for children.

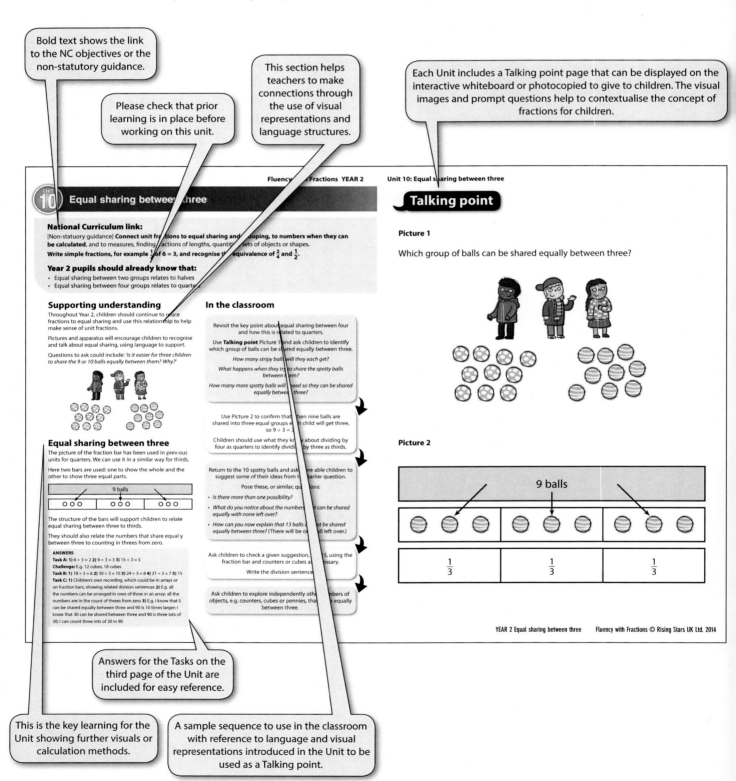

Answers for the Tasks on the third page of the Unit are included for easy reference.

This is the key learning for the Unit showing further visuals or calculation methods.

A sample sequence to use in the classroom with reference to language and visual representations introduced in the Unit to be used as a Talking point.

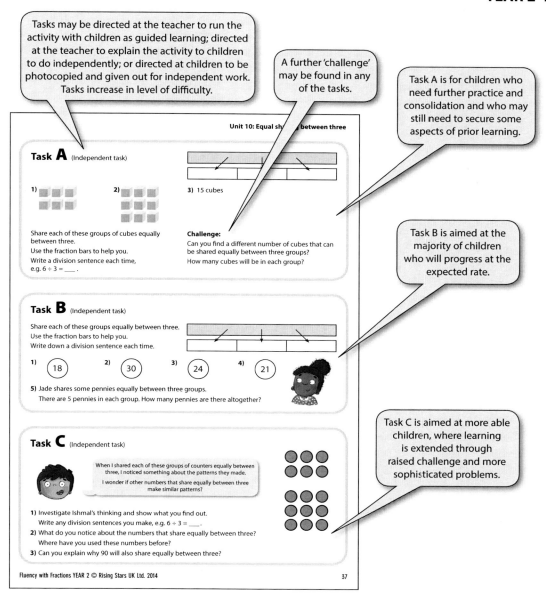

Tasks may be directed at the teacher to run the activity with children as guided learning; directed at the teacher to explain the activity to children to do independently; or directed at children to be photocopied and given out for independent work. Tasks increase in level of difficulty.

A further 'challenge' may be found in any of the tasks.

Task A is for children who need further practice and consolidation and who may still need to secure some aspects of prior learning.

Task B is aimed at the majority of children who will progress at the expected rate.

Task C is aimed at more able children, where learning is extended through raised challenge and more sophisticated problems.

Curriculum mapping grid

The grid below shows in which Units objectives from the 2014 National Curriculum Programme of Study for Year 2 are covered. Note that objectives are revisited regularly and learning progressed in subsequent units. In the National Curriculum link section of each Unit, bold text is used to indicate which specific part of the overarching objective is addressed within the Unit, since objectives often cover a range of different knowledge and skills (particularly for younger age groups).

Objectives	Unit														
	1	2	3	4	5	6	7	8	9	10	11	12	13	14	15
Count in fractions up to 10, starting from any number and using the $\frac{1}{2}$ and $\frac{2}{4}$ equivalence on the number line.	✔							✔	✔						
Connect unit fractions to equal sharing and grouping, to numbers when they can be calculated, and to measures, finding fractions of lengths, quantities, sets of objects or shapes.		✔								✔					
Recognise, find, name and write fractions $\frac{1}{3}$, $\frac{1}{4}$, $\frac{2}{4}$ and $\frac{3}{4}$ of a length, shape, set of objects or quantity.			✔		✔	✔	✔				✔	✔	✔	✔	✔
Write simple fractions, for example $\frac{1}{2}$ of 6 = 3, and recognise the equivalence of $\frac{2}{4}$ and $\frac{1}{2}$.			✔	✔	✔	✔	✔	✔		✔		✔	✔		✔

UNIT 1 Counting and combining halves

National Curriculum link:

[Non-statutory guidance] **Count in fractions up to 10, starting from any number and using the $\frac{1}{2}$ and $\frac{2}{4}$ equivalence on the number line.**

Year 2 pupils should already know that:

- A set of objects shared equally between two results in two groups of an equal size
- Halving gives the same result as sharing equally between two
- Two halves combine to equal a whole

Supporting understanding

Through previous work, children should already know that halving gives the same result as sharing equally between two.

We can also describe this relationship in a different way, e.g. two halves of apple are equal to a whole apple so four halves of apple are equal to two whole apples.

Familiar pictures and everyday contexts should be used to secure this relationship and then extended to include combining quarters in later units.

> There are **two** halves in a whole so **two** halves can be combined to equal a whole.

Counting and combining halves

As children progress to calculating with fractions in Key Stage 2, knowledge of the fractions that combine to equal a whole is vital. Counting supports this concept.

> There are **two** halves in **one** whole so there are **six** halves in **three** of these wholes.

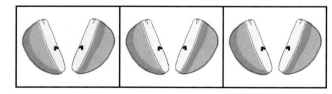

The picture here shows how halves are combined as we count.

In the classroom

> Revisit the key point that halving gives the same result as sharing equally between two and that two halves can be put together to equal a whole.

> Use **Talking point** Picture 1.
>
> *Do you think this shows halving? How do you know?*
>
> Discuss the number of halves that can be seen and then describe them.
>
> Use this language: *'There are two halves of apple in one whole apple so there are six halves of apple in three whole apples.'*

> Count in halves to confirm and model using the pictures of fruit.
>
> Pose questions for different groups to think about:
> - *How many halves have we counted?*
> - *How many wholes is that?*
> - *When I stop at four halves, how many wholes have we counted?*
> - *How many more apples will I need for eight halves?*

> Use Picture 2 to show the apple halves in a fraction bar.
>
> Ask children to explain why the picture has been arranged in this way, why some areas are shaded and why some lines are thicker.

> Count in halves along the picture to show that every two halves equal another whole.
>
> *What must we do to show eight halves of apple?*

ANSWERS

Task A: 1) Something to show that she can cut 12 halves, e.g. fraction bar or pictures **2)** 8 halves so 4 whole apples

Task B: 1) 6 **2)** 3 **3)** 2 **4)** 5 **5)** Fraction bar showing 16 halves

Task C: 1) Fraction bars showing 14 halves, 18 halves, etc. (must require an odd number of whole apples) **2)** 22 halves so 11 whole apples; she cannot have 24 halves as we know she uses an odd number of apples

Talking point

Picture 1

Do the apples show halving? How do you know?

There are ____ halves of apple in ____ whole apples.

Picture 2

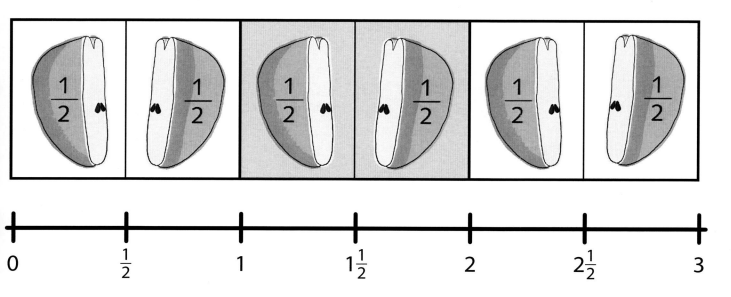

Unit 1: Counting and combining halves

Task A (Guided learning with an adult)

Gran is cutting apples to make an apple pie.

I only have **6** apples.
How many halves can I cut?

1) Help Gran with her problem.

Write or draw something to show what you have found out.

2) Gran used this fraction bar to help her.

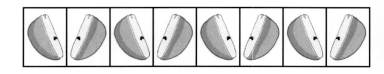

How many halves did she cut?

How many whole apples did she use?

Task B (Independent task)

Gran is cutting apples to make an apple pie.
She draws this fraction bar to help her.

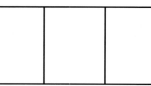

1) How many halves of apple can you see?

2) How many whole apples has Gran cut so far?

3) How many more whole apples does Gran need to fill the fraction bar?

4) Count up to two wholes and a half on the fraction bar. How many halves have you counted?

5) Draw the fraction bar Gran used to help her cut eight apples.

Write $\frac{1}{2}$ on each piece and practise counting in halves.

Task C (Independent task)

Gran is cutting apples to make an apple pie.
She uses an odd number of apples.

There are more than **12** halves for my pie.

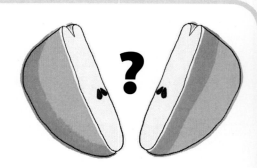

1) Draw two different fraction bars to show the possible number of halves of apple Gran used for her pie.

How many whole apples did she use each time?

2) Gran used less than 13 apples.

What is the greatest number of halves of apple she can have?

Count in halves to check.

UNIT 2

Finding out more about equal sharing between four

National Curriculum link:

[Non-statutory guidance] **Connect unit fractions to equal sharing and grouping**, to numbers when they can be calculated, and to measures, finding fractions of lengths, quantities, sets of objects or shapes.

Year 2 pupils should already know that:

- A set of objects shared equally between four results in four groups of an equal size
- Finding a quarter gives the same result as sharing equally between four
- Halving gives the same result as sharing equally between two

Supporting understanding

The work that children will have done about fractions builds on the principle of sharing equally. It is just as important for children to appreciate 'unequal sharing' so that they recognise when they have made errors in their fraction work.

Continue to use activities, pictures and apparatus to encourage children to recognise and talk about equal sharing, using language to support.

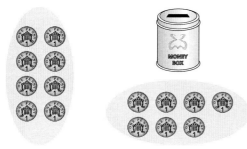

Questions to ask could include: *'Is it easier for four children to share the 8p or 7p equally between them? Why?'*

Equal sharing between four

The picture of the fraction bar has been used in Unit 1 and also in Year 1.

Here three bars are used; one to show the whole and the other two to show four equal parts.

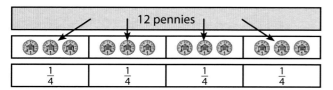

The structure of the bars will support children to make the link between equal sharing between four and quarters.

ANSWERS
Task A: B (20) and C (16) share equally **Challenge:** 4, 8, 12, 24, etc.
Task B: Children's own recordings to show that every four added will result in the total sharing equally between four
Challenge: E.g. 'Yes, because 8 shares equally between 4 and 80 is 10 times bigger'
Task C: 1) $12 \div 4 = 3$, $20 \div 4 = 5$, $28 \div 4 = 7$, etc. with corresponding fraction bars **2)** E.g. Jade cannot have used 32 because $32 \div 4 = 8$ and 8 is an even number

In the classroom

Use **Talking point** Picture 1 to introduce the problem.

Jade wants to find out about sharing equally between four. She decides to use the coins in her money box.

She is excited to find out that her pennies can be shared equally into four groups.

Which pennies belong to Jade? How do you know? What can you show me? How many pennies would be in each group?

Which pennies do not belong to Jade? How do you know?

Consider Picture 2.

What does this show? How do you know?

Establish that it shows Jade's 12 pennies shared into four equal groups. There are four equal groups of 3 so we can write $12 \div 4 = 3$. There are four quarters in a whole so one quarter is worth three pennies.

Return to the 11 pennies.

Pose these, or similar, questions:

- *How many more pennies will I need so they can be shared equally between four?*
  Is there more than one possibility?

- *How can you explain that 13 cannot be shared equally between four?*

Ask children to check a given suggestion, using the fraction bar and pennies as necessary.

Write the division sentence.

Ask children to explore independently other numbers of pennies that share equally between four.

Refer to quarters when discussing work with groups.

Talking point

Picture 1

Which group of coins belongs to Jade?

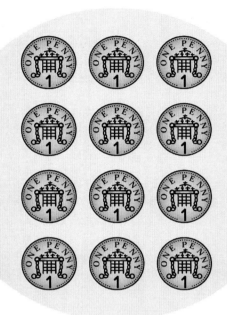

Picture 2

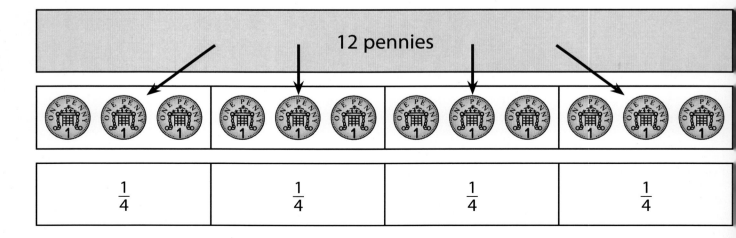

Task A (Independent task)

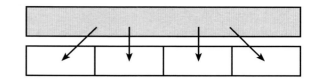

Which numbers of pennies share equally between four? Use the fraction bar to help you.

A)
MONEY BOX
15

B)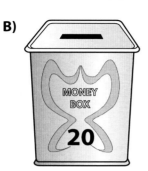
MONEY BOX
20

C)
MONEY BOX
16

D)
MONEY BOX
18

Challenge:

Can you find a different number of coins that Jade can share equally between four groups?
How many pennies will be in each?

Task B (Guided learning with an adult)

I know that **4** pennies share equally between **four** groups.

I think that every time I put another **4** pennies in my money box, I can always share all the pennies in the box between **four** groups!

MONEY BOX

Use fraction bars to help you investigate Jade's thinking.
Write the division sentences each time.

Challenge:

Do you think that 80 pennies can be shared equally between four? Why?

Task C (Independent task)

When I tried sharing different numbers of pennies equally between four, all the groups I made had an odd number of pennies in them!

MONEY BOX

1) Use fraction bars to help you find out some possible numbers of pennies Jade used.

   Write matching division sentences each time.

2) How can you explain why Jade cannot have started with 32 pennies?

UNIT 3 Finding different quarters of a shape

National Curriculum link:

Recognise, find, name and write fractions $\frac{1}{3}$, $\frac{1}{4}$, $\frac{2}{4}$ and $\frac{3}{4}$ of a length, shape, set of objects or quantity.

Write simple fractions, for example $\frac{1}{2}$ of 6 = 3, and **recognise the equivalence of $\frac{2}{4}$ and $\frac{1}{2}$**.

Year 2 pupils should already know that:

*   A set of objects shared equally between four results in four groups of an equal size
*   Finding quarters gives the same result as sharing equally between four

Supporting understanding

Children have been exploring equal sharing between four and have identified the numbers that can be shared easily, e.g. 4, 8, 12,16, 20. They recognise that when odd numbers are shared between two, there is one left over, so when odd numbers are shared between four there are some left over.

This unit develops the idea of equal sharing to quarters and supports children in recognising a number of quarters in shape.

One whole divided into **four** equal parts.

Each part is worth $\frac{1}{4}$.

Finding quarters

Find and share pictures that show an object or a group of objects shared equally between four, e.g:

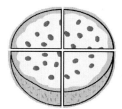

Encourage children to discuss what they notice, including how many quarters they see in the whole.

Make sure to establish the 'equal sharing' and the 'equal parts' that result. Each part is worth one quarter so two parts are worth two quarters, etc.

ANSWERS

Task A: It is not possible to cut the circle in different ways; of others, octagon is most challenging

Task B: 1) All shapes folded and labelled **2)** $\frac{1}{4}$ of a labelled square shaded **3)** Two quarters of a labelled hexagon shaded to show this is equal to $\frac{1}{2}$ **4)** Two different examples of a rectangle in quarters with $\frac{3}{4}$ shaded on each

Task C: There is more than one solution as long as the first shape has only $\frac{1}{4}$ shaded, the last has none or all four quarters shaded and the others fit the rules given, e.g. $\frac{1}{4}$ hexagon, $\frac{2}{4}$ $\left(\frac{1}{2}\right)$ square, $\frac{2}{4}$ $\left(\frac{1}{2}\right)$ octagon, $\frac{3}{4}$ square, $\frac{3}{4}$ circle, $\frac{4}{4}$ circle

In the classroom

Remind children of some of the work they have been doing about equal sharing between four.

How do we know that we have shared a group of objects equally between four?

Reinforce that finding quarters is the same as equal sharing between four and the result is four equal parts.

Ask children to visualise a square or a circle and then visualise cutting it equally in four to make quarters.

Children could sketch or fold shapes, share with each other and check the number of equal parts that they have.

Use **Talking point** Picture 1 for children to compare and agree different ways that quarters can be shown. Children may have other examples.

Pose these, or similar, questions:

*   *Do any of the shapes look like the ones you saw and drew?*
*   *I think that both the circles show quarters. Do you agree? Why?*
*   *I think that both the squares show quarters. Do you agree? Why?*

Use the pictures of the two squares to prove that all the quarters are the same size even though they may not all look the same. You can do this by taking the $\frac{1}{4}$ strips in the second square, cutting them in half and placing them on the quarters in the first square.

Count in quarters up to a whole, remembering to think about the equivalence of a half and two quarters.

Now consider Picture 2, the octagon. This is also in quarters, but some of them are shaded.

How many parts are shaded? How many quarters is this?

Establish that three quarters are shaded, as three quarters out of four quarters are shaded. Write this as $\frac{3}{4}$.

Talking point

Picture 1

Which shapes show quarters?

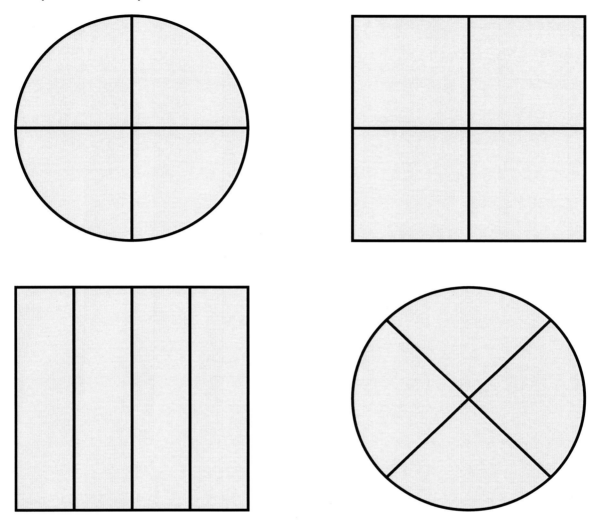

Picture 2

How many quarters are shaded?

Unit 3: Finding different quarters of a shape

Task **A** (Independent task)

You will need these paper shapes.
Sally is finding out about quarters.
She has pictures of each of these shapes.

I think I can find two different ways to find quarters of each of these shapes.

What do you think?

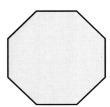  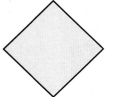 

Find a way to show what you have found out. Label your quarters each time.

Task **B** (Independent task)

You will need several of these paper shapes.
Pete is finding out more about different numbers of quarters.
He has these shapes.

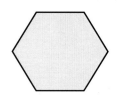

1) Take one of each of Pete's shapes. Fold them into quarters and label them.

2) Shade $\frac{1}{4}$ of the square.

3) Shade 2 quarters of the hexagon. Describe the amount shaded in a different way.

4) Pete used two rectangles. He shaded $\frac{3}{4}$ in two different ways.
   Show how he might have done this.

Task **C** (Guided learning with an adult)

Abi put six shapes in a line to make a pattern.
These are the shapes she used to help her.
Use the clues to find the pattern she made.
You can use more than one of each shape.
Is there more than one possible pattern?

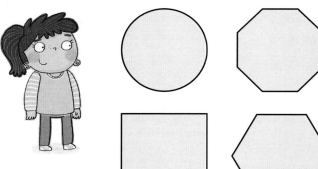

- Two different shapes have $\frac{3}{4}$ shaded.
- Identical shapes show quarters drawn in different ways.
- Two different shapes have $\frac{1}{2}$ shaded, with each shape folded in quarters.
- The first shape in the pattern only has $\frac{1}{4}$ shaded.
- The last shape in the pattern does not have the same amount shaded as any of the other shapes.

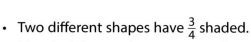
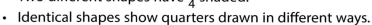

Fluency with Fractions YEAR 2 © Rising Stars UK Ltd. 2014

UNIT 4 Fractions of a turn and equivalence

National Curriculum link:
Write simple fractions, for example $\frac{1}{2}$ of 6 = 3, and **recognise the equivalence of $\frac{2}{4}$ and $\frac{1}{2}$.**

Year 2 pupils should already know that:
- We use fractions to describe parts of a whole and also turns
- We can use equal sharing to help us make sense of fractions
- We can count the number of fractions in a whole

Supporting understanding
Using a range of pictures will help children to recognise relationships between some of the fractions they are using, including equivalent fractions. Half and two quarters are the first equivalent fractions that children meet.

In this unit children will look at turns and link these to their work on fractions. In Year 2 they build on their understanding of quarter, half and three-quarter turns.

There are **two** quarters of a turn in a **half** turn.

Equivalence
Children should explore a range of pictures that clearly show that $\frac{1}{2}$ is equal to $\frac{2}{4}$.

Work on equivalence will also support understanding when counting in steps of $\frac{1}{4}$ up to 10, including numbers such as $1\frac{1}{4}$, $1\frac{2}{4}$ (or $1\frac{1}{2}$), $1\frac{3}{4}$, etc. This is set out in the non-statutory guidance for Year 2 and will be covered in Unit 9.

ANSWERS
Task A: 1) $\frac{1}{4}$ **2)** 10 **3)** $\frac{1}{4}$ **4)** 20 **5)** 2 quarters is equal to 1 half
Challenge: 3 quarter turns; 30 points
Task B: 1) $\frac{1}{4}$ **2)** 5 **3)** Two quarter turns **4)** 15 **5)** 2 and $\frac{1}{2}$ turns or 2 and $\frac{2}{4}$ turns **Challenge:** E.g. $1\frac{1}{4}$ turns score 25 points
Task C: 1) $1\frac{1}{4}$, 2 full, $1\frac{1}{2}$, $1\frac{3}{4}$ **2)** E.g. six $\frac{1}{4}$ turns or three $\frac{1}{2}$ turns for 150 points, ten $\frac{1}{4}$ turns or five $\frac{1}{2}$ turns for 250 points

In the classroom
Revisit the key point that we can use fractions to describe parts of a whole turn.

Look at **Talking point** Picture 1. The solid arrow shows the direction that Tom is facing. He wants to turn so that he faces the direction of the dashed arrow.

What should he do? Does it matter which way he turns?

Establish that he can make a clockwise or anti-clockwise half turn (or rotation).

Pose a question for children to consider whether he could have made this turn in a different way:

What if he made more than one turn? What can you tell me now? How do you know?

Use this language: 'There are **two** quarters of a turn in a **half** turn.'

Ask children to check the turn themselves, moving as necessary.

Now children should imagine Tom making a full turn.

How many different ways can he make a whole turn?

Extend more able children to consider two full or whole turns.

Ask children to explore ideas. These should include four quarter turns, one half turn and two quarter turns and two half turns.

Look at Picture 2.

Tom decides to use what he knows about turns to help him when he plays the 'Spinning Wheel' game with Abi.

A full or whole turn will score 24 points.

How can we use this information to find out how many points Tom and Abi scored on their first go?

On their last go, Abi scored eight points more than Tom.

How many ways can you make this true?

How can you describe the turns each child made?

Talking point

Picture 1

What fraction of a whole turn do I need to make?

How should Tom turn to face the dashed arrow?

Picture 2

How many points did Abi and Tom score on their first go?

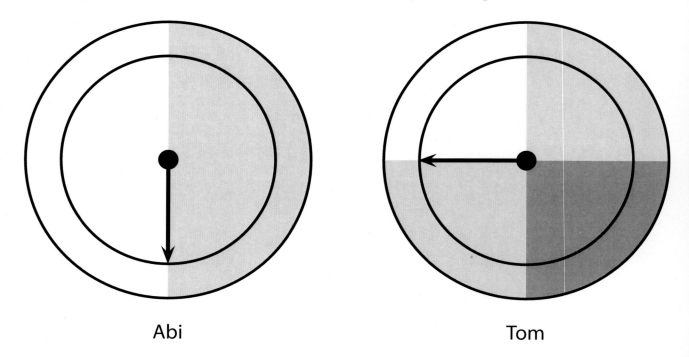

Abi   Tom

Task **A** (Guided learning with an adult)

Use a paper plate, a paper arrow and a split pin to make the 'Spinning Wheel' game.

A whole turn in the game is worth 40 points. Turn your arrow so it matches the spinning wheel shown.

1) What fraction of a turn have you made so far?

2) How many points have you scored?

Now continue to turn your arrow so it shows $\frac{1}{2}$ a turn.

3) What fraction of a turn did you have to make?

4) How many points have you scored now?

5) Copy and complete: 2 quarters is equal to ___ .

Challenge:
Find out about $\frac{3}{4}$ of a turn. How many quarter turns is this? How many points will you score?

Task **B** (Independent task)

Use a paper plate, a paper arrow and a split pin to make the 'Spinning Wheel' game.

Izzy also plays the 'Spinning Wheel' game. Her spinning wheel is shown.
A whole turn in the game is worth 20 points.

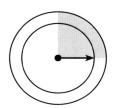

1) What fraction of a turn has Izzy made so far?

2) How many points has she scored?

3) Izzy makes another $\frac{1}{2}$ of a turn. How many quarter turns does she have to make?

4) How many points does she now have altogether?

5) Izzy scored 50 points altogether. What can you tell me about the turns she made?

Challenge:
Explore some other turns that are more than a whole turn and write the number of points you score.

Task **C** (Independent task)

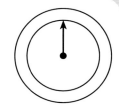

Use a paper plate, a paper arrow and a split pin to make the 'Spinning Wheel' game.
Here are the five games of 'Spinning Wheel' that Pete played.
A whole turn in the game is worth 100 points.

Game 1	Game 2	Game 3	Game 4	Game 5
125 points	200 points	150 points	175 points	

1) What turns did Pete make in each game?

2) In Game 5, Pete turned the wheel an even number of quarter turns. He could also have made the same turn with an odd number of half turns. He scored more than 100 points.

What turns could Pete have made? Find at least two possible solutions.

UNIT 5 Linking quarters to time

National Curriculum link:

Recognise, find, name and write fractions $\frac{1}{3}$, $\frac{1}{4}$, $\frac{2}{4}$ **and** $\frac{3}{4}$ **of a length, shape, set of objects or quantity.** Write simple fractions, for example $\frac{1}{2}$ of 6 = 3, and **recognise the equivalence of** $\frac{2}{4}$ **and** $\frac{1}{2}$.

Year 2 pupils should already know that:

- A set of objects shared equally between four results in four groups of an equal size
- Finding quarters gives the same result as sharing equally between four

Supporting understanding

In Year 2, children will experience finding halves and quarters in number work and in measurement, and will also use these to describe direction and movement.

We can also make this link to time: 'Tell and write the time to five minutes, including quarter past / to the hour and draw the hands on a clock face to show these times.'

Children find time more difficult as there is more than one scale, i.e. the hours as 1 to 12, and minutes and seconds as 0 to 60.

Language structures will help children to talk more confidently about time and make links in learning.

> The minute hand has gone a **quarter** of the way around the clock. It is quarter past …

Quarter of an hour

The pictures below show quarters in three different ways.

The one on the left will be used with Year 2 children to help them recognise 'quarter past' the hour.

'Quarter to' is a little more tricky. The picture in the middle shows 'quarter of an hour' and can be later used to represent time intervals.

The one to the right shows that the minute hand has moved $\frac{3}{4}$ of the way around the clock (supporting e.g. 1:45 in Year 3) and there is still $\frac{1}{4}$ of an hour to go to complete the hour. It is 'quarter to …'.

ANSWERS
Task A: Children's sorting of clocks in table
Task B: 1) E.g. quarter past 9, quarter past 10, quarter past 2, quarter past 3 **2)** Quarter to 3 **3)** E.g. quarter to 10, quarter to 11, etc. (linked to answers to question 1)
Task C: E.g. Ishmal: quarter past 1, quarter to 2 and quarter to 5; Abi: quarter past 2, half past 2 (both later than Ishmal's first times) and quarter to 3; there are other solutions as long as Ishmal writes quarter to 5, Abi writes quarter to 3 and the rest of the times fit the given criteria

In the classroom

Using **Talking point** Picture 1, of a circle and a clock, ask children to discuss what is the same and what is different.

What do you think the shaded part shows?

What do you think I am trying to show on my clock?

Use a clock resource to show an o'clock time, e.g. 12 o'clock.

Pose these, or similar, questions for groups to think about:

- *How long will it take before my clock shows another o'clock time? How can I describe this, as a turn?*
- *What fraction of a whole turn will the minute hand make as it moves from 12 to 6? What time is this?*
- *What fraction of a whole turn will the minute hand make as it moves from 12 to 3? What time is this?*

First, model the minute hand moving all the way around to complete a whole hour or full turn. Consider a half turn and then a quarter turn.

Use this language: *'The minute hand has gone a quarter of the way around the clock. It is quarter past … '.*

Ask children to give examples.

Now consider Picture 2 in the same way. Children should discuss the similarities between the amount shaded on the circle and on the clock. They should also think about what the clock could be showing.

Starting from 12 o'clock, model the minute hand moving one quarter, then two quarters (same as one half) and then three quarters of the way around the clock.

It has made $\frac{3}{4}$ of a turn, but it has not yet completed a full turn.

Establish that there is still one quarter of a turn left to go to reach the next hour (o'clock) and this can be described as 'quarter to …'. This is 'quarter to one' in the example, as there is a quarter of an hour to go until 1 o'clock.

Talking point

What do the shaded parts show?

Picture 1

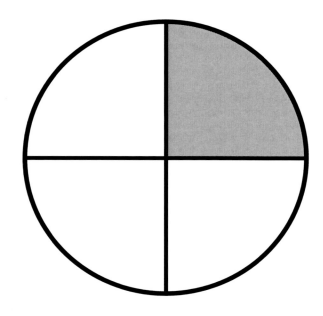 

Picture 2

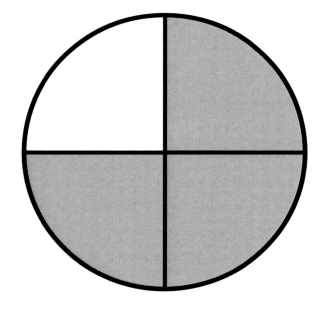 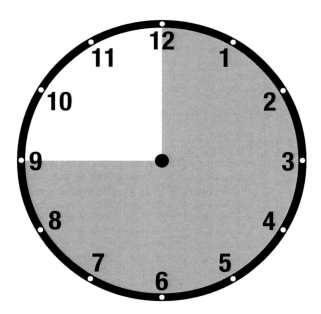

Task **A** (Independent task)

Provide children with a range of cut-out clocks showing 'half-past' and 'quarter-past' times.

Half past	Quarter past

The minute hand has gone ____ way around the clock.

It is ____ past ____ .

Ask children to sort the clocks onto a pre-drawn table and use the language in the speech bubbles to describe any of the times they find.

Provide children with a few blank clocks and challenge them to add a time of their own to either part of the table.

Task **B** (Independent task)

You will need some clock resources.

Class 2 are writing down all the times in the school day where the minute hand has moved quarter of the way around the clock, like the picture here.

1) Use the clocks below to show and write four different times for Class 2.

2) Jade's clock shows a quarter past two. She moves the minute hand anoter two quarters of the way around the clock. What is the time now?

There is a quarter of an hour still to go to reach ____ o'clock. It is quarter to ____ .

3) Now use your clocks from question 1 and move the minute hand in the same way as Jade. Write the new times you make.

Task **C** (Guided learning with an adult)

You will need some clock resources.

Ishmal and Abi are finding out more about quarters to help them tell the time.

They each write down three **different** times between 1 o'clock and 5 o'clock.

Which times did they write down?

Use the clues to help you.

Is it possible to find more than one solution?

CLUES:
- None of the times are o'clock times.
- Ishmal writes down two times. One time is half an hour later than the other.
- Abi also writes down two times. Both these times are later than the ones Ishmal wrote down.
- The third time that Ishmal writes means there is still quarter of an hour to go before 5 o'clock.
- Abi's third time is exactly two hours earlier than Ishmal's third time.

UNIT 6
Finding different quarters of a group of objects

National Curriculum link:

Recognise, find, name and write fractions $\frac{1}{3}$, $\frac{1}{4}$, $\frac{2}{4}$ and $\frac{3}{4}$ **of a length, shape, set of objects or quantity. Write simple fractions, for example** $\frac{1}{2}$ **of 6 = 3, and recognise the equivalence of** $\frac{2}{4}$ **and** $\frac{1}{2}$.

Year 2 pupils should already know that:

- A set of objects shared equally between four results in four groups of an equal size
- Finding quarter gives the same result as sharing equally between four

Supporting understanding

Children should have plenty of practical experience of finding a half and a quarter of a shape, object or group of objects.

In previous units they looked in more depth at the relationship between halves and quarters and how three quarters combine to equal $\frac{3}{4}$.

Language structures to emphasise 'equal sharing' should continue to be used here.

> I know that I have found **quarters** because I have **four** equal groups. A **quarter** of 20 is 5.

Finding different quarters of a group

To find the fraction of an amount or a set of objects, we must view the set as the 'whole', i.e. the whole set or whole amount.

Fraction bars and other pictures can be used to show how the 'whole' can be split into fractions.

1 whole			
$\frac{1}{4}$	$\frac{1}{4}$	$\frac{1}{4}$	$\frac{1}{4}$

In the context of the 'whole' as 20 sweets, the following picture arises:

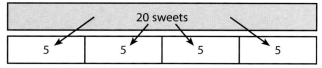

We can now see how much each quarter is worth and use this to find the value of more than one quarter, e.g. $\frac{3}{4}$.

Remember that halving and halving again provides an alternative strategy to sharing equally between four.

ANSWERS
Task A: 1) 2 **2)** 3 **3)** 5 **4)** 4 **5)** $\frac{2}{4}$ is 4 and $\frac{3}{4}$ is 6
Task B: 1) Incorrect: $\frac{1}{4}$ of 24 = 6 **2)** Correct **3)** Incorrect: $\frac{3}{4}$ of 16 is 12 **4)** $\frac{3}{4}$ of 8 is 6 **5)** E.g. $\frac{3}{4}$ of 40 is 30
Task C: 1) Children's work to show finding a quarter each time and then calculating three of these, so e.g. $\frac{1}{4}$ of 40 = 10 so $\frac{3}{4}$ of 40 is three lots of 10 = 30 **2)** E.g. $\frac{1}{4}$ of 40 = 10 so 40 − 10 = 30 and this is the same as three lots of $\frac{1}{4}$, or $\frac{3}{4}$

In the classroom

Use **Talking point** Picture 1 to introduce the problem to be developed:

Sid and Bonnie work at the park. They are busy planting flowers, but they cannot decide how many they need to plant in each section of the flower bed so all the flowers are shared equally.

Ask children to discuss what they know about equal sharing and give some examples in response to:

What if there are two sections in the bed? What if there are four sections?

Show Picture 2 and pose questions for different groups to consider:

- *How many equal groups do they need to make? What do we call these fractions?*
- *How many flowers need to be planted in each section? How do you know?*
- *Sid thinks it should be four flowers in each part. Explain why he has made a mistake.*

Label each section of the bed as $\frac{1}{4}$, counting the quarters to agree that there are four equal parts.

Use equal sharing and Picture 2 to model 20 ÷ 4 = 5.

The language structure (in the speech bubble to the left) will also be useful here.

Show that the same result can be found by halving 20 and then halving again.

Sid starts by planting $\frac{1}{4}$ of the flowers. Record this as $\frac{1}{4}$ of 20 = 5.

But what fraction has been planted when Bonnie plants another quarter? How many flowers is this?

Record this as $\frac{2}{4}$ of 20 = 10 and $\frac{1}{2}$ of 20 = 10 using the equivalence between two quarters and a half.

Use Picture 3 to show the relationship between the more contextual Picture 2 and the fraction bars.

Ask children to discuss what the picture is showing and the number of flowers planted in $\frac{3}{4}$ of the bed.

Talking point

Picture 1

Can you plant an equal number of flowers in each section of the flower bed?

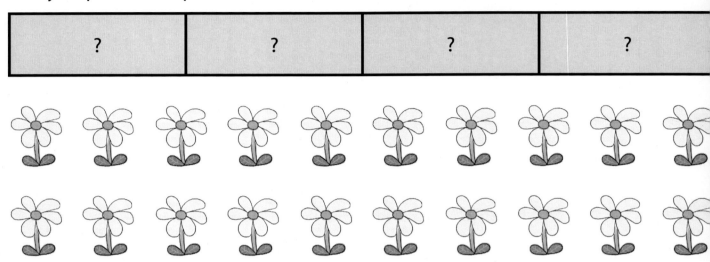

Picture 2

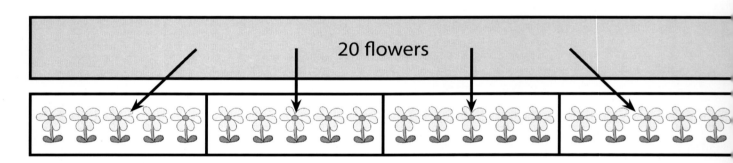

Picture 3

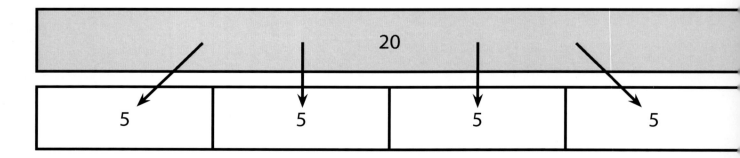

Task A (Independent task)

Sid and Bonnie have more flowers to plant. The flower beds always show quarters.

$\frac{1}{4}$	$\frac{1}{4}$	$\frac{1}{4}$	$\frac{1}{4}$

Find $\frac{1}{4}$ of each of these groups of flowers. Show what you have found out.

1)
8

2)
12

3)
20

4)
16

5) Now find $\frac{2}{4}$ of 8 flowers. Can you also find $\frac{3}{4}$ of 8 flowers?

Task B (Independent task)

Sid and Bonnie planted lots of flowers that day. This is what Sid wrote about the different fractions they planted:

1) $\frac{1}{4}$ of a group of 24 flowers is 5.

2) $\frac{2}{4}$ of a group of 24 flowers is 12.

3) $\frac{3}{4}$ of a group of 16 flowers is 8.

Check Sid's work. Is he correct? Explain any mistakes he has made.

4) $\frac{3}{4}$ of a group of ___ flowers is 6.

5) $\frac{3}{4}$ of a group of ___ flowers is ___ .

Finish sentence 4) for Sid. Make up your own example for sentence 5).

Task C (Independent task or guided learning with an adult)

Bonnie has been finding different quarters of these groups of flowers.

1) Prove to Bonnie that she can always find $\frac{3}{4}$ of a group by finding $\frac{1}{4}$ and then counting three of these quarters.

2) Sid thinks he has a better idea.

What do you think?
Explore Sid's idea and then find a way to prove your thinking.

To find $\frac{3}{4}$ of each group of flowers, we only need to take $\frac{1}{4}$ of them away from the number in the whole group!

40

24

100

80

UNIT 7 Using fractions to compare measurements

National Curriculum link:

Recognise, find, name and write fractions $\frac{1}{3}$, $\frac{1}{4}$, $\frac{2}{4}$ and $\frac{3}{4}$ of a length, shape, set of objects or quantity. Write simple fractions, for example $\frac{1}{2}$ of 6 = 3, and recognise the equivalence of $\frac{2}{4}$ and $\frac{1}{2}$.

Year 2 pupils should already know that:

- Two quarters combine to equal one half
- We compare groups of objects or quantities using what we know about fractions, e.g. 5p is half of 10p

Supporting understanding

Within measurement, Year 2 children should be taught to 'choose and use appropriate standard units to estimate and measure'. Non-statutory guidance states that 'Comparing measures includes simple multiples such as "half as high"; "twice as wide".'

In this unit, children will be comparing the mass of objects and finding out about different fractions of a mass.

Object 1   Object 2

> I know that object 2 weighs **half** of object 1 because **5 kg** is **half** of **10** kg.

Using fractions to compare mass

Fraction bars or other pictures can also be used to explore and compare mass.

We can compare the objects in the example above using two bars.

10 kg	Object 1

5 kg	5 kg	Object 2

Therefore, $\frac{1}{2}$ of 10 kg = 5 kg.

ANSWERS

Task A: 1) 6 kg, 8 kg, 10 kg, 7 kg **2)** 3 kg

Task B: 1) $\frac{1}{2}$ of 40 kg = 20 kg, $\frac{1}{2}$ of 50 kg = 25 kg, $\frac{1}{2}$ of 30 kg = 15 kg, $\frac{1}{2}$ of 24 kg = 12 kg **2)** $\frac{1}{4}$ each time: 10 kg, 20 kg and 40 kg are the missing values

Task C: 1) Recorded as $\frac{1}{4}$ of … ; missing values are 100 kg, 80 kg, 25 kg, 36 kg **2)** Different fractions, e.g. $\frac{1}{4}$ of 80 kg = 20 kg, $\frac{3}{4}$ of 20 kg = 15 kg and even $\frac{1}{3}$ of 15 kg = 5 kg

In the classroom

Use **Talking point** Picture 1 to introduce the concept of using fractions with measurement.

What do we know about the mass of the object on each scale? How can we compare the masses using fractions? What else can you tell me? (E.g. $\frac{1}{2}$ of 10 kg is 5 kg or double 5 kg is 10 kg.)

Use the language structure to support understanding.

Show Picture 2 and ask children how this is related to the picture they saw before. What is the same? What is different?

Establish that it helps us to compare the fractions and that we can also write this as $\frac{1}{2}$ of 10 kg = 5 kg.

Ask children to discuss the mass of other objects that can be weighed on this scale and that can also be compared using the fraction 'half'.

Ask more able children to think about objects that can be weighed on this scale also using the fraction 'half', e.g. 5 kg and 2$\frac{1}{2}$ kg.

Pose questions such as:

- *Object 1 weighs 8 kg; what can you tell me about object 2?*
- *Object 1 weighs 70 g; what can you tell me about object 2?*

Return to 8 kg as the mass of object 1.

If object 2 weighs only 2 kg, what fraction can we use to compare them now?

A Cuisenaire 8 rod can be used to find out how many 2 rods equal it.

There are four equal parts so each is $\frac{1}{4}$.

Record this as $\frac{1}{4}$ of 8 kg = 2 kg.

We know this is correct because two quarters is 2 kg + 2 kg, which is equal to a half of 8 kg.

Talking point

Picture 1

What do the objects weigh?

Object 1

Object 2

Picture 2

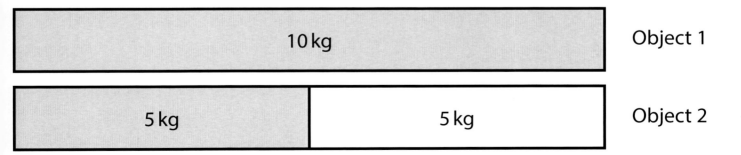

| 10 kg | | Object 1 |
| 5 kg | 5 kg | Object 2 |

Task A (Guided learning with an adult)

In Sami's book, the mass of two objects is compared.

Object 2 is always half of the mass of object 1.

1) Here are some of the masses of the different objects he compared.

   Find the missing mass each time.

   Use the speech bubble to help you.

I know that object 2 weighs **half** of object 1 because ___.

Object 1	12 kg	16 kg	20 kg	14 kg
Object 2				

2) The mass of object 1 this time is 12 kg, but object 2 only weighs a $\frac{1}{4}$ of it.

   What is the mass of object 2?

Task B (Independent task)

In Sami's book, the mass of two objects is compared.

Object 2 is always half of the mass of object 1.

1) Here are some of the mass he compared.

   Find the missing mass each time.

   Compare objects using a number sentence, e.g. $\frac{1}{2}$ of ___ = ___ .

Object 1	40 kg	50 kg	30 kg	24 kg
Object 2				

2) Abi has also been comparing masses.

   What fraction can she use to compare the objects this time? Find the missing masses.

Object 1	16 kg	40 kg		
Object 2	4 kg		5 kg	10 kg

Task C (Independent task)

 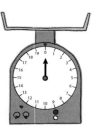

In Sami's book, the mass of two objects is compared.

Object 2 is always a quarter of the mass of object 1.

1) Here are some of the masses he compared.

   Find the missing mass each time.

   Compare objects using a number sentence, e.g. $\frac{1}{4}$ of ___ = ___ .

Object 1	400 kg		100 kg	
Object 2		20 kg		9 kg

2) Abi has also been comparing different objects.

   What fractions can she use to compare these masses? Record the number sentences you use.

   20 kg **5 kg** **15 kg**

   40 kg **80 kg** **60 kg**

I think I can compare them using $\frac{3}{4}$ as my fraction!

UNIT 8 Combining halves and quarters in measurement

National Curriculum link:

Write simple fractions, for example $\frac{1}{2}$ of 6 = 3, and recognise the equivalence of $\frac{2}{4}$ and $\frac{1}{2}$.

[Non-statuory guidance] Count in fractions up to 10, starting from any number and using the $\frac{1}{2}$ and $\frac{2}{4}$ equivalence on the number line.

Year 2 pupils should already know that:

- Two halves combine to equal a whole and four quarters combine to equal a whole
- Two quarters combine to equal a half

Supporting understanding

Year 2 non-statutory guidance indicates that children count in fraction steps of halves and quarters up to 10. As part of this counting they will also need to apply knowledge of combining two quarters to equal a half.

Developing the use of pictures, e.g. fraction bars, can help children to recognise and use this relationship.

Combining halves and quarters

Using pictures and practical experiences, children should recognise the result of combining halves and quarters, including as parts of a whole.

Problem solving contexts encourage children to make decisions. Children will firstly consider the fraction in each container and then explore the result of combining some of these fractions.

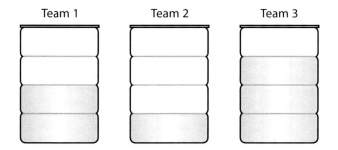

Team 1   Team 2   Team 3

ANSWERS

Task A: Children's own responses

Task B: E.g. $\frac{1}{2}$ and $\frac{1}{2}$; $\frac{1}{4}$, $\frac{1}{4}$ and $\frac{1}{2}$, four quarters ; children's own recording

Task C: 1) Children record, using fractions, how much each runner collects and what is in the container after each runner; runner 1 collects less than a quarter and runner 2 collects more than a quarter of the container **2)** Team 4: $\frac{4}{4}$ or has a full container; Team 5: $\frac{3}{4}$

In the classroom

Using **Talking point** Picture 1, of three containers, introduce the problem that will be developed:

Three teams are collecting water in a race on Sports Day.

What can you tell me about the fraction of water each team has collected in their container? How do you know?

Develop the language children use with structures such as: *'I think … because …'* and *'I know it is a quarter because …'*, to help secure understanding.

Label each container.

Team 2 puts some more water in their container so they have the same amount as Team 1.

Pose these, or similar, questions for different groups to think about:

- *What fraction will be in Team 2's container now?*
- *What fraction did Team 2 add to their container?*
- *How can you write a fraction to show the water in the container now? Can we write it in two different ways?* ($\frac{1}{2}$ and $\frac{2}{4}$)

Establish and model that two quarters combine and this is the same as a half. Picture 2 shows what happened.

In the last part of the race, Team 1 doubles the amount of water in their container and Team 3 fills their container.

What can you tell me now?

How can you describe the fraction of water that Team 3 put in their container in the last part of the race?

Use pictures to confirm and model ideas, establishing (for Team 1) that two halves combine to equal one whole.

Talking point

Picture 1

What can you tell me about the fraction of water each team has collected in their container? How do you know?

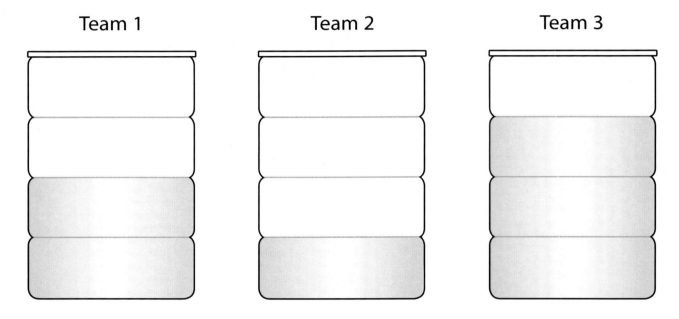

Picture 2

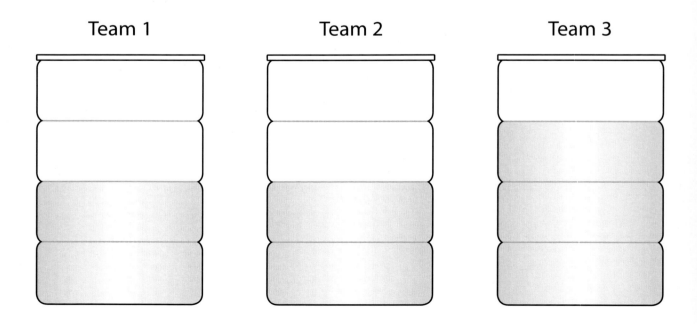

Task **A** (Guided learning with an adult)

Work together on a practical task to model the events of the race considered in the main lesson.

Start with three identical empty containers.

Ask children to estimate and represent the water shown in Picture 1 and then add the water described at different stages of the problem.

Ask children to think about:

• how to describe and write the fraction each time.

• what fraction Team 2 still needs to collect to fill their container.

> I think ___ because ___.

> I know it is a **quarter** because ___.

Task **B** (Independent task)

Team 4 ran in the next race. They also filled their container but they did not fill it in one go.

• Use containers and water to investigate the different fractions they collected and in what order.

• How many different ways can you find?

• Show what you find out.

?

Task **C** (Independent task)

Team 4 and Team 5 ran in the next race.

Team 4   Team 5

?   **?**

1) Use your containers and water to find out what happened.

Find out how much water each runner collects and how much water is in the container each time.

	Runner 1	Runner 2	Runner 3	Runner 4
Team 4	Collected water that filled less than a quarter of the container	Collected enough water to half-fill the container	Put in another $\frac{1}{4}$ of the container	Fills the container
Team 5	Collected water that filled exactly $\frac{1}{4}$ of the container	Collected no water	Collected enough water to half-fill the container	After runner 4, the team still needs $\frac{1}{4}$ to fill the container

2) What fraction has each team collected at the end of the race?

Counting in fraction steps of $\frac{1}{2}$ and $\frac{1}{4}$ beyond 1

UNIT 9

National Curriculum link:

[Non-statutory guidance] **Count in fractions up to 10, starting from any number and using the $\frac{1}{2}$ and $\frac{2}{4}$ equivalence on the number line.**

Year 2 pupils should already know that:

- Two halves are equivalent to a whole and four quarters are equivalent to a whole
- Two quarters are equivalent to one half

Supporting understanding

Useful models provide a clear link between fractions of a whole and where these fractions sit on a number line.

Fractions of a whole shown only as 'pizzas', etc. can be limiting and become missed opportunities when making links.

Consider the use of a 'bar' to show the number of quarters in a whole:

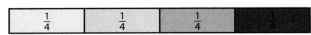

We can also count the number of quarters represented as a running total:

(or a whole)

This can easily be shown as part of a number line, so reinforcing the key point that fractions are numbers and can be placed on a number line:

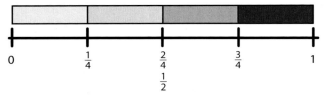

Fractions greater than 1

There is often a misconception that fractions are part of 1 that results in children struggling with the notion of mixed and improper fractions in Key Stage 2. The picture above can easily be extended to show that fractions extend beyond 1:

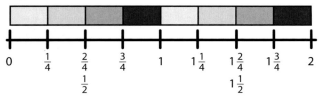

ANSWERS

Task A: Children label fraction bars and record their findings

Task B: Children construct number lines

Task C: Alice: steps of $\frac{1}{4}$ (look for children who recognise that eight lots of $\frac{1}{4}$ are equal to 2); Ishmal: does not land on zero but on $\frac{1}{4}$; Billy: landed on 6, or $1\frac{1}{2}$ if he counted back; Sanra: any starting place that is a whole number or includes $\frac{1}{2}$, e.g. $1\frac{1}{2}$, 2, $2\frac{1}{2}$

In the classroom

Revisit the key point that two halves are equivalent to a whole and four quarters are equivalent to a whole.

Use familiar (but identical-sized) pictures to reinforce this.

The **Talking point** picture of two houses can be used here. The windows represent fraction bars.

Invite children to count the number of halves and quarters they can see in a window. Use the language: *'I can count one half, two halves, so there are two halves in a whole,'* etc.

Use the identical pictures and the result of the quarters count to reinforce the key point that two quarters are equivalent to one half.

Use the pictures to link the previous language sentence to the running total of halves and then the running total of quarters.

Pose these, or similar, questions for different groups to consider:

- *What will happen when I add another 'window' of halves? How many halves will we count then?*

- *What will happen when I add another 'window' of quarters? How many quarters will we count then? How can we record the running total of quarters on a fraction bar?*

Link the fraction bar 'window' of halves to the picture of the number line, then add the second 'window' to show how the count is extended.

Invite children to create their own number line for quarters and discuss how the count extends when a second, and then a third, 'window' is added.

Rehearse counting in halves, up to at least 3 on the number line initially.

Repeat with quarters, but ensure that when e.g. $1\frac{2}{4}$ is counted, a group of designated 'Half Hunters' count this as $1\frac{1}{2}$.

Talking point

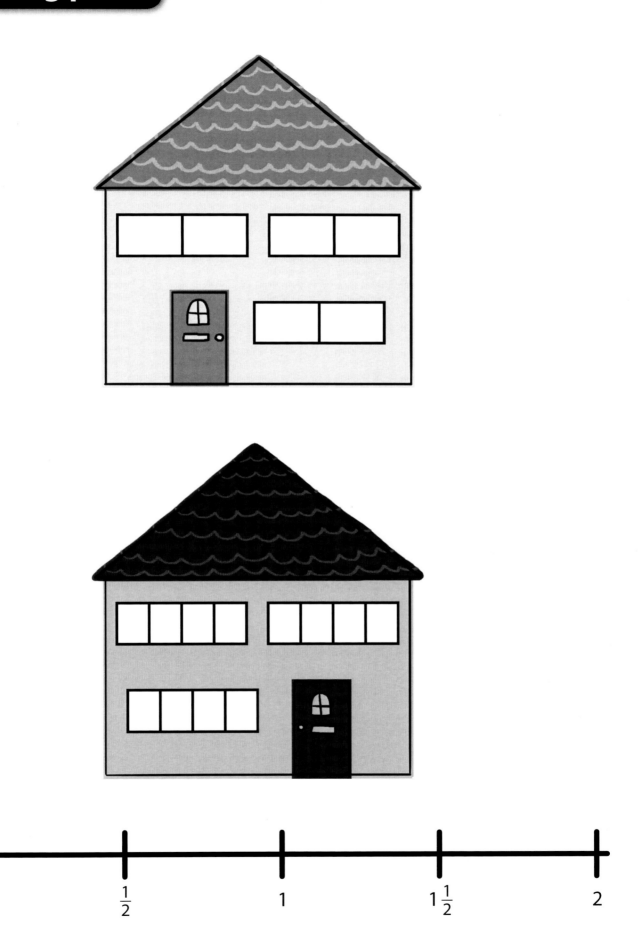

Task **A** (Independent task)

Ask children to work in pairs with four 'halves' fraction bars.

They should label each half and then discuss the number of halves they can see in each whole and how many they can see altogether.

Ask children to record their findings in their own way or in a table as follows:

	Number of wholes	Number of halves
▢▢		
▢▢ ▢▢		
▢▢ ▢▢ ▢▢		
▢▢ ▢▢ ▢▢ ▢▢		

Task **B** (Independent task)

▢▢▢▢ ▢▢▢▢ ▢▢▢▢ ▢▢▢▢

Work in pairs with four fraction bars as shown.

Label each quarter and then discuss the number of quarters you can see in each whole and how many you can see altogether.

Using a strip of paper or border roll (longer than all four fraction bars placed side by side), construct and label your own number lines showing the count of quarters from 0 to at least 4.

0	$\frac{1}{4}$	$\frac{2}{4}$	$\frac{3}{4}$	1	$1\frac{1}{4}$
	$\frac{1}{4}$	$\frac{1}{4}$	$\frac{1}{4}$	$\frac{1}{4}$	

Task **C** (Guided learning with an adult)

Alice, Ishmal, Billy and Sanra are all talking about the counting they have been doing.

Alice

> I counted 8 steps on my number line. I started at $2\frac{1}{2}$ and stopped on $4\frac{1}{2}$. What can you tell me about my step size?

Ishmal

> I started on $5\frac{3}{4}$ and counted back in halves. Did I land on zero?

Billy

> I counted in steps of $\frac{1}{4}$. I started on $3\frac{3}{4}$ and made 9 steps. Where did I stop?

Sanra

> I also counted back in halves, but I did land on zero! How many ways can you make this true?

Draw number lines to show what you know about each child's counting.

UNIT 10 Equal sharing between three

National Curriculum link:

[Non-statuory guidance] **Connect unit fractions to equal sharing and grouping, to numbers when they can be calculated**, and to measures, finding fractions of lengths, quantities, sets of objects or shapes.

Write simple fractions, for example $\frac{1}{2}$ of 6 = 3, and recognise the equivalence of $\frac{2}{4}$ and $\frac{1}{2}$.

Year 2 pupils should already know that:

- Equal sharing between two groups relates to halves
- Equal sharing between four groups relates to quarters

Supporting understanding

Throughout Year 2, children should continue to relate fractions to equal sharing and use this relationship to help make sense of unit fractions.

Pictures and apparatus will encourage children to recognise and talk about equal sharing, using language to support.

Questions to ask could include: *'Is it easier for three children to share the 9 or 10 balls equally between them? Why?'*

Equal sharing between three

The picture of the fraction bar has been used in previous units for quarters. We can use it in a similar way for thirds.

Here two bars are used: one to show the whole and the other to show three equal parts.

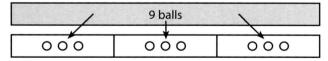

9 balls

The structure of the bars will support children to relate equal sharing between three to thirds.

They should also relate the numbers that share equally between three to counting in threes from zero.

ANSWERS
Task A: 1) 6 ÷ 3 = 2 **2)** 9 ÷ 3 = 3 **3)** 15 ÷ 3 = 5
Challenge: E.g. 12 cubes, 18 cubes
Task B: 1) 18 ÷ 3 = 6 **2)** 30 ÷ 3 = 10 **3)** 24 ÷ 3 = 8 **4)** 21 ÷ 3 = 7 **5)** 15
Task C: 1) Children's own recording, which could be in arrays or on fraction bars, showing related division sentences **2)** E.g. all the numbers can be arranged in rows of three in an array; all the numbers are in the count of threes from zero **3)** E.g. I know that 9 can be shared equally between three and 90 is 10 times larger; I know that 30 can be shared between three and 90 is three lots of 30; I can count three lots of 30 in 90

In the classroom

Revisit the key point about equal sharing between four and how this is related to quarters.

Use **Talking point** Picture 1 and ask children to identify which group of balls can be shared equally between three.

How many stripy balls will they each get?

What happens when they try to share the spotty balls between them?

How many more spotty balls will I need so they can be shared equally between three?

Use Picture 2 to confirm that when nine balls are shared into three equal groups each child will get three, so 9 ÷ 3 = 3.

Children should use what they know about dividing by four as quarters to identify dividing by three as thirds.

Return to the 10 spotty balls and ask more able children to suggest some of their ideas from the earlier question.

Pose these, or similar, questions:

- *Is there more than one possibility?*

- *What do you notice about the numbers that can be shared equally with none left over?*

- *How can you now explain that 13 balls cannot be shared equally between three?* (There will be one ball left over.)

Ask children to check a given suggestion, e.g. 15, using the fraction bar and counters or cubes as necessary.

Write the division sentence.

Ask children to explore independently other numbers of objects, e.g. counters, cubes or pennies, that share equally between three.

Talking point

Picture 1

Which group of balls can be shared equally between three?

Picture 2

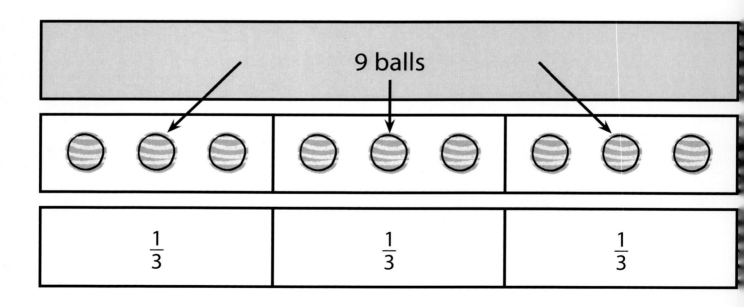

Task **A** (Independent task)

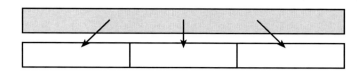

1)    2) 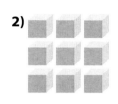   3) 15 cubes

Share each of these groups of cubes equally between three.

Use the fraction bars to help you.

Write a division sentence each time, e.g. 6 ÷ 3 = ___ .

Challenge:

Can you find a different number of cubes that can be shared equally between three groups?

How many cubes will be in each group?

Task **B** (Independent task)

Share each of these groups equally between three.
Use the fraction bars to help you.
Write down a division sentence each time.

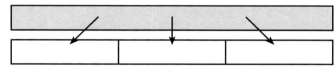

1) 18   2) 30   3) 24   4) 21

5) Jade shares some pennies equally between three groups. There are 5 pennies in each group. How many pennies are there altogether?

Task **C** (Independent task)

When I shared each of these groups of counters equally between three, I noticed something about the patterns they made.

I wonder if other numbers that share equally between three make similar patterns?

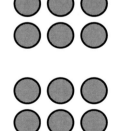

1) Investigate Ishmal's thinking and show what you find out.
   Write any division sentences you make, e.g. 6 ÷ 3 = ___ .

2) What do you notice about the numbers that share equally between three?
   Where have you used these numbers before?

3) Can you explain why 90 will also share equally between three?

UNIT 11 Finding a third of a shape

National Curriculum link:

Recognise, find, name and write fractions $\frac{1}{3}$, $\frac{1}{4}$, $\frac{2}{4}$ and $\frac{3}{4}$ of a length, shape, set of objects or quantity.

Year 2 pupils should already know that:

- When a shape is divided into two equal parts, each part is called a half $\left(\frac{1}{2}\right)$
- When a shape is divided into four equal parts, each part is called a quarter $\left(\frac{1}{4}\right)$
- Two halves combine to equal a whole and four quarters combine to equal a whole

Supporting understanding

Children have been exploring equal sharing between three and have identified numbers that can be equally shared with none left over, e.g. 3, 6, 9, 12. They recognise that these can be odd or even.

This unit develops the connection of equal sharing between three with thirds, and helps children to recognise thirds in shape.

One whole divided into **three** equal parts.

Each part is worth $\frac{1}{3}$.

Finding thirds of a shape

Find and share pictures that show different shapes divided into thirds. Flags of the world are useful.

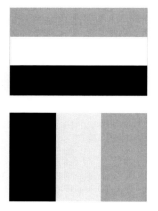

Encourage children to discuss what they notice, including how many thirds they see in the whole.

It is also useful to look at dividing a circle into thirds, to support work in upper Key Stage 2 when children will need to interpret pie charts. It also supports the position of the minute hand for 20 past and 20 to the hour.

In the classroom

Remind children of some of the work they have been doing about equal sharing between three.

How do we know that we have shared a group of objects equally between three?

Reinforce that finding thirds is the same as equal sharing between three and the result is three equal parts.

Ask children to visualise a rectangle and then visualise cutting it equally in three to make thirds.

Children could sketch or fold shapes, share with each other and check the number of equal parts that they now have.

Use **Talking point** Picture 1 to show how fractions are all around us. Ask children to compare the flags with some of their own ideas.

Pose these, or similar, questions:

- *Do any of the shapes look like the ones you saw and drew? How do you know?*
- *I think that all the flags show thirds. Do you agree? Why?*
- *What mistake do you think I have made? Why?*

Using the flag of The Netherlands or Belgium, check that there are three equal parts. It would be useful to fold one of the pictures along the lines to check that they are all equal.

Count and label thirds up to a whole.

Now look at Picture 2, of a clock, and ask different groups to consider these questions:

- *How many parts can you see?*
- *Do you think they are all equal?*
- *I think that this also shows thirds. Do you agree?*
- *How do you know that these three parts are equal? How can we use what we know about time to help us?*

Establish that we can find thirds of other shapes, but it is not always easy.

ANSWERS
Task A: Shapes sorted by criteria; children add a shape of their own
Task B: E.g. 'thirds' group includes a circle, rectangle, square and hexagon; 'not thirds' group includes a triangle, and three other shapes either with three unequal parts or showing different fractions, e.g. quarters; yes, there

are more solutions as we can keep adding shapes to each group; there are several ways that thirds can be shown on e.g. a rectangle
Task C: E.g. 'thirds' group includes a hexagon, semi-circle, circle and square; 'not thirds' group and other solutions as for Task B; 'not thirds' group also includes a shape with quarters

Talking point

Picture 1

The Netherlands

Czech Republic

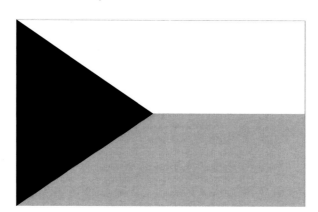

Belgium

Chile

Picture 2

Task A (Independent task)

You will need a range of shapes showing thirds and not thirds, e.g:

   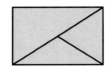 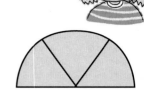

1) Sort the shapes into groups, as shown in the table.
2) Now look at the shapes in thirds.
   Label each part as $\frac{1}{3}$.
3) Can you find another way to show a rectangle or square in thirds? Add it to your group.

Thirds $\left(\frac{1}{3}\right)$	Not thirds $\left(\frac{1}{3}\right)$

Task B (Guided learning with an adult)

Izzy sorted different shapes into the groups shown in the table.
Use the clues to help you find out what happened.

Thirds $\left(\frac{1}{3}\right)$	Not thirds $\left(\frac{1}{3}\right)$

- There is an equal number of shapes in each group.
- Some of the shapes she used were squares, rectangles, circles and triangles.
- She put the only hexagon in the 'thirds' group.
- She used more than six shapes altogether.

Find a way to make this true. Label any thirds you make.

Do you think there could be more than one solution? Explain your thinking.

Task C (Independent task)

Izzy sorted different shapes into the groups shown in the table.
Use the clues to help you find out what happened.

Thirds $\left(\frac{1}{3}\right)$	Not thirds $\left(\frac{1}{3}\right)$

CLUES:
- There is an equal number of shapes in each group.
- She put the only hexagon in the 'thirds' group.
- She put the only semi-circle in the 'thirds' group.
- Izzy also used squares, circles and triangles.
- One of Izzy's shapes shows quarters.
- She used more than six shapes altogether.

Find a way to make this true. Label any thirds you make.

Do you think there could be more than one solution? Explain your thinking.

UNIT 12 Finding a third of a quantity (length)

National Curriculum link:

Recognise, find, name and write fractions $\frac{1}{3}$, $\frac{1}{4}$, $\frac{2}{4}$ and $\frac{3}{4}$ of a length, shape, set of objects or quantity.

Write simple fractions, for example $\frac{1}{2}$ of 6 = 3, and recognise the equivalence of $\frac{2}{4}$ and $\frac{1}{2}$.

Year 2 pupils should already know that:

- A set of objects shared equally between three results in three groups of an equal size
- Unit fractions relate to equal sharing

Supporting understanding

Children should have plenty of practical experience of finding a fraction of a group of objects, of a shape and of a measurement.

In previous units, children related thirds to sharing equally between three. They will draw on this knowledge to find $\frac{1}{3}$ of lengths.

Language structures to emphasise 'equal sharing' should continue to be used here.

> I know that I have found **thirds** because I have **three** equal parts.

> A **third** of **12** cm is **4** cm.

Finding a third of a length

Cuisenaire rods, integer bars or paper strips can be used to help children investigate fractions of length. Centimetre squares in books can also support here.

Consider Cuisenaire rods used to represent 12. This is also 12 cm in length, as Cuisenaire rods are designed as centimetre rods (e.g. white 1 cm, red 2 cm, etc.).

10 cm + 2 cm

In this example, we know that a third can be found by equal sharing between three so we need to find three equal lengths (rods) that are the same length as 12 cm.

10 cm + 2 cm

| 4 cm | 4 cm | 4 cm |

We can clearly see that $\frac{1}{3}$ of 12 cm = 4 cm as 12 cm ÷ 3 = 4 cm.

ANSWERS

Task A: 1) $\frac{1}{3}$ of 6 cm = 2 cm **2)** $\frac{1}{3}$ of 9 cm = 3 cm **3)** $\frac{1}{3}$ of 15 cm = 5 cm
Challenge: $\frac{1}{3}$ of 30 cm = 10 cm
Task B: 1) $\frac{1}{3}$ of 30 cm = 10 cm **2)** $\frac{1}{3}$ of 21 cm = 7 cm **3)** $\frac{1}{3}$ of 24 cm = 8 cm
4) $\frac{1}{3}$ of 33 cm = 11 cm **5–7)** Children should relate this to the thirds they found in the class session, so $\frac{1}{3}$ of 12 m = 4 m, etc. **Challenge:** 33 cm
Task C: 1) $\frac{1}{3}$ of 60 cm = 20 cm **2)** $\frac{1}{3}$ of 36 cm = 12 cm **3)** $\frac{1}{3}$ of 300 cm = 100 cm **4)** $\frac{1}{3}$ of 75 cm = 25 cm **5)** 90 m **6)** 36 m **7)** 45 m
Challenge: Children's examples should show these are equal; both are 8

In the classroom

Revisit the key point that unit fractions are connected to equal sharing.

What does that tell us about $\frac{1}{3}$?

Ask children to give an example of sharing equally between three, perhaps linked to work in previous units.

Use **Talking point** Picture 1.

We need to find $\frac{1}{3}$ of each of these lengths of patterned paper so that they can be shared equally between three children for their art project.

What can we do? It is quite tricky to fold into thirds.

Ask children to discuss possible strategies and feed back ideas. Link to sharing equally between three.

Share Picture 2. Suggest that $\frac{1}{3}$ of 12 cm can be found by finding three equal lengths that are the same length in total as 12 cm.

Children should check this suggestion using Cuisenaire rods, integer bars or 1 cm squared paper, along with a ruler.

Pose this question for different groups to consider:

How can we use the same idea to help us find $\frac{1}{3}$ of 15 cm? Of 18 cm?

Write children's findings as $\frac{1}{3}$ of 12 = 4, $\frac{1}{3}$ of 15 = 5, etc. and relate to language, e.g:

'I know that I have found thirds because I have three equal parts. A third of 12 cm is 4 cm.'

In the independent tasks, children will explore $\frac{1}{3}$ of different lengths, including metres.

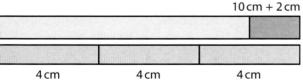

Talking point

Picture 1

How can we find a third?

12 cm

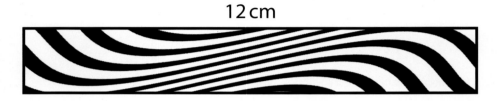

15 cm

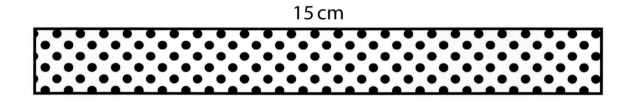

18 cm

Picture 2

10 cm + 2 cm

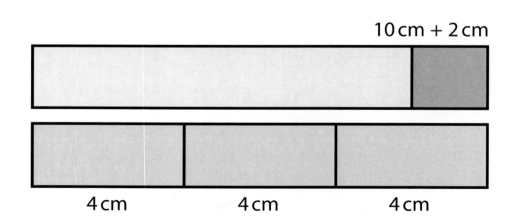

4 cm   4 cm   4 cm

Task **A** (Independent task)

Use practical equipment to explore finding $\frac{1}{3}$ of each of these lengths.

Write what you find out each time using $\frac{1}{3}$ of ___ cm = ___ cm.

1) | 6 cm |

2) | 9 cm |

3) | 15 cm |

HINT: Remember to give your answers in centimetres.

Challenge:

Make a 30 cm length and then find $\frac{1}{3}$ of it.

Task **B** (Independent task)

Use practical equipment to explore finding $\frac{1}{3}$ of each of these lengths.

Write what you find out each time using $\frac{1}{3}$ of ___ cm = ___ cm.

1) 30 cm   **2)** 21 cm   **3)** 24 cm   **4)** 33 cm

Use what you know to help you find $\frac{1}{3}$ of these lengths.

5) 12 metres   **6)** 15 metres   **7)** 18 metres

HINT: Remember to give your answers in centimetres or metres.

Challenge:

Pete cuts a paper strip into thirds. Each of his thirds is 11 cm long.
What was the length of the whole paper strip?

Task **C** (Guided learning with an adult)

Find $\frac{1}{3}$ of each of these lengths.
Write what you find out each time using $\frac{1}{3}$ of ___ cm = ___ cm.

1) 60 cm   **2)** 36 cm   **3)** 300 cm   **4)** 75 cm

Sami is also finding out about thirds.
Copy and complete each of Sami's fraction sentences.

5) $\frac{1}{3}$ of ___ = 30 m   **6)** $\frac{1}{3}$ of ___ = 12 m   **7)** $\frac{1}{3}$ of ___ = 15 m

Challenge:
Which is larger: $\frac{1}{3}$ of 24 cm or $\frac{1}{4}$ of 32 cm?
Prove your thinking.

UNIT 13 Problems about finding thirds (measurement)

National Curriculum link:

Recognise, find, name and write fractions $\frac{1}{3}$, $\frac{1}{4}$, $\frac{2}{4}$ and $\frac{3}{4}$ of a length, shape, set of objects or quantity. Write simple fractions, for example $\frac{1}{2}$ of 6 = 3, and recognise the equivalence of $\frac{2}{4}$ and $\frac{1}{2}$.

Year 2 pupils should already know that:

- A set of objects shared equally between three results in three groups of an equal size
- Equal sharing between three groups relates to thirds
- When we count from zero in threes, the numbers in our count can be shared equally between three with nothing left over

Supporting understanding

Earlier work has provided children with opportunities to apply understanding of fractions to practical contexts and make links to real-life situations.

In this unit, children apply thirds to money. This is mainly in pounds, but also extends to 50 pence pieces for more able children.

Pictures such as fraction bars or other shapes showing thirds will support children when calculating.

Solving problems

It is important that children have plenty of opportunities to apply knowledge and skills. This not only secures understanding but also provides evidence of learning.

To be successful, children must first make sense of the problem and find a starting point. Encourage children to tell the story of the problem, role-play it or sketch something that helps them to make sense of it.

As teachers, we need to model how to be a problem solver and show children how to find starting points.

> What do I need to find out?

> What do I already know?

> How does this help me?

ANSWERS
Task A: E.g. spent £3 so £9 in box, spent £4 so £12 in box
Challenge: £10
Task B: E.g. $\frac{1}{3}$ of £18 = £6, $\frac{1}{3}$ of £21 = £7 **Challenge:** No, because $\frac{1}{3}$ of an odd number is always odd; $\frac{1}{3}$ of an even number is even
Task C: E.g. Pete £1 and 50p and Izzy £4 and 50p; least amount is Pete 50p and Izzy £1 and 50p; greatest amount is Pete £9 and 50p and Izzy £28 and 50p

In the classroom

Revisit the key point that equal sharing between three groups relates to thirds.

Use **Talking point** Picture 1 to introduce the problem that will be developed during the main part of the lesson:

Jade and Ishmal have only pound coins. Jade has less than £13.
- *Jade has $\frac{1}{3}$ of the money she needs for Gran's present.*
- *Ishmal has $\frac{1}{3}$ of the money he needs for Grandpa's present.*
- *Jade has half the amount of money that Ishmal has.*

Ask children to suggest ways to solve the problem.
Give different groups different tasks, e.g:

1) *If Jade has £1, what do we know about the whole amount needed for Gran's present? What if Jade has £2? Or £3?*
2) *Using what you know, explore possible amounts for Ishmal.*
3) *(For more able children) Explore the possible amounts that Jade and Ishmal have, using the last clue to help you.*

Come back together to share what has been found out so far. The groups exploring either Jade or Ishmal's amounts should explain any patterns they notice.

Jade has $\frac{1}{3}$ of the money she needs for Gran's present.
What is the largest amount she can have? Why?
And Ishmal? Why?

Ask the groups who were exploring different possible amounts Jade and Ishmal can have to share their ideas.

Ask more able children to feed back on their findings and explain why Ishmal cannot have $\frac{1}{3}$ of £18 when Jade has $\frac{1}{3}$ of £12.

Agree some possible solutions (record as $\frac{1}{3}$ of ___ = ___) and use **Talking point** Picture 2 to confirm the solution where Jade and Ishmal have the least amounts of money.

Ask children to describe the picture for the greatest possible amounts of money.

Children will be helping Jade's friend Izzy in the independent tasks.

Talking point

Picture 1

How could you solve the problem?

Jade and Ishmal have only pound coins.
Jade has less than £13.

Jade has $\frac{1}{3}$ of the money she needs
for Gran's present

Ishmal has $\frac{1}{3}$ of the money he needs
for Grandpa's present

Jade has half the amount of money
that Ishmal has.

Picture 2

Ishmal

$\frac{1}{3}$ of £6 = £2

Jade

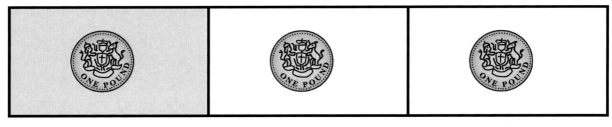

$\frac{1}{3}$ of £3 = £1

Unit 13: Problems about finding thirds (measurement)

Task **A** (Guided learning with an adult)

Izzy spends $\frac{1}{3}$ of the money in her money box on a present for Gran.
She only has pound coins.

I spent more than **two** pound coins on the present.

Use coins to find out the different amounts Izzy could have spent on Gran's present and the total number of pound coins in her money box each time.

Challenge:

Izzy had £30 in her money box. How much did Gran's present cost?

Task **B** (Independent task)

Izzy spends $\frac{1}{3}$ of the money in her money box on a present for Gran.
She only has pound coins.

I spent more than **five** pound coins on the present.

Find out the different amounts Izzy could have spent on Gran's present and the total number of pound coins in her money box each time.
Write a number sentence each time.

Challenge:

Izzy had an odd number of coins in her money box before she bought the present.
Can Gran's present have cost an even number of coins?
Prove your thinking.

Task **C** (Independent task or guided learning with an adult)

Izzy and Pete have only pound coins and 50 pence pieces.

- Pete has less than £10.
- Pete has $\frac{1}{3}$ of the amount of money that Izzy has.
- Pete always has a 50 pence piece.

1) How much do Izzy and Pete each have? Find some different solutions.

2) Find a solution where each child has the least amount of money possible.

3) Find a solution where each child has the greatest amount of money possible.

HINT: Making lists will help you.

UNIT 14 Finding fractions of quantities (measurement)

National Curriculum link:
Recognise, find, name and write fractions $\frac{1}{3}$, $\frac{1}{4}$, $\frac{2}{4}$ and $\frac{3}{4}$ of a length, shape, set of objects or quantity.

Year 2 pupils should already know that:
- Unit fractions are connected to equal sharing
- Fractions are numbers and can be placed on the number line
- Two quarters are equivalent to a half

Supporting understanding
Measurement provides valuable opportunities to recognise, combine and count in fractions.

Children in Year 2 work with standard units of measurement, including litres and millilitres.

Children should use the language of fractions and measurement to help them explain and make decisions.

> I know it is a **quarter** of a litre because I can see that **4** of them will equal **1** litre.

Fractions of capacity
Using pictures and practical experiences, children should recognise halves and quarters when working with capacity and volume.

Problem solving contexts encourage children to make decisions, e.g: *Does each of these containers hold $\frac{1}{4}$ litre?*

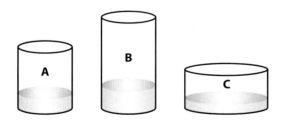

In this example, children will need to look carefully as none of the containers are the same size. They should learn that they must compare the fraction to the whole, in this case 1 litre.

ANSWERS
Task A: Challenge: A second jug is needed; one full jug and a second jug with $\frac{1}{4}$ litre in it
Task B: 1) Holds 4 litres (which is double 2 litres) **2)** 1 litre because there are two halves in a whole **3)** 3 **4)** 0, $\frac{1}{2}$ litre, 1 litre, 1$\frac{1}{2}$ litres, 2 litres, 2$\frac{1}{2}$ litres **5)** 0, $\frac{1}{4}$ litre, $\frac{2}{4}$ litre $\left(\frac{1}{2}\right)$, $\frac{3}{4}$ litre, etc. 2$\frac{2}{4}$ litre $\left(2\frac{1}{2}\right)$
6) All the numbers in the $\frac{1}{2}$ litre count are in the $\frac{1}{4}$ litre count
Task C: 1) As for Task B **2)** 1$\frac{1}{2}$ litres **3)** 5 **4)** 0, $\frac{1}{4}$ litre, $\frac{2}{4}\left(\frac{1}{2}\right)$ litre, etc. 2$\frac{3}{4}$ litres **5)** 2$\frac{3}{4}$ is not in the count; it only has $\frac{1}{2}$ and wholes **6)** E.g. from $\frac{1}{4}$ or $\frac{3}{4}$

In the classroom

> Remind children that fractions help us with measurement.
>
> Using **Talking point** Picture 1, ask children to discuss and explain what fraction of each container is full.
>
> *If each container can hold 1 litre, could each one in my picture have $\frac{1}{4}$ of a litre of water in it? Why?*

> Discuss what has made this task a little more difficult: none of the containers are the same shape.
>
> Establish that we must look at the fraction compared to the whole and decide whether it is a quarter or not.
>
> Use this language: '*I know it is a quarter of a litre because I can see that four of them will equal 1 litre*' and '*I know it is not a quarter because ....*'
>
> Look for children who refer to four equal parts.

> Establish that all containers do have $\frac{1}{4}$ litre of water.
>
> Pose these, or similar, questions for different groups to think about:
>
> - *How much water will be in my jug when I pour in the water from containers A and B? How many quarters of a litre is this?*
>
> - *How much water will be in my jug when I pour in the water from all my containers?*
>   *What fraction of a litre will I still need to fill my jug?*
>   *Why can this fraction not be $\frac{1}{3}$ of a litre?*

> Explore children's ideas using language structures and practical modelling to help explain.
>
> Look at **Talking point** Picture 2.
>
> *What is different about this jug? What is the same?*
>
> *What will happen when I pour the water from my first jug into this one?*
>
> Introduce container D (containing $\frac{1}{2}$ litre).
>
> Ask children to discuss different ways to fill the rest of the jug with water. Count in quarters and halves up to 2 litres.

Talking point

Picture 1

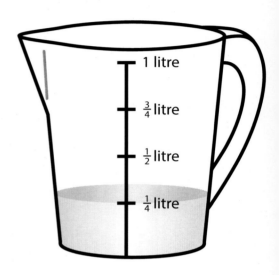

Picture 2

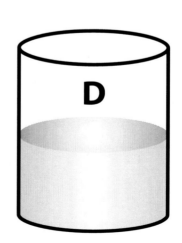

Task **A** (Independent task)

Work in pairs or a small group to investigate ways of filling a 1 litre jug.
Use containers that hold $\frac{1}{4}$ litre and $\frac{1}{2}$ litre of water.

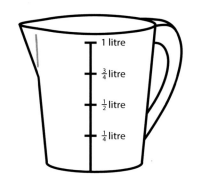

Think about:
- how to describe and write the fraction each time you add more water.
- what fraction of a litre still needs to be added to fill the jug each time.

Challenge:
Fill your jug to $\frac{3}{4}$ litre.
What will you need to do so that you can add another $\frac{1}{2}$ litre without spilling any water?
Describe what you have now.

Task **B** (Guided learning with an adult)

1) What can you tell me about the container this time?
2) When I pour two lots of $\frac{1}{2}$ litre of water into the empty container, where will
   the water come up to? How do you know?
3) How many more lots of $\frac{1}{2}$ litre of water will we need to match the water
   level shown here?
4) Count in $\frac{1}{2}$ litres from zero up to the water level shown here.
   Write down your count.
5) How can I count from zero up to the same level in $\frac{1}{4}$ litres?
   Write down your count.
6) Which numbers were in both of your counts? Why?

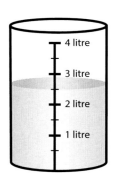

Task **C** (Independent task)

1) What can you tell me about the container this time?
2) When I pour three lots of $\frac{1}{2}$ litre into the empty container, where will the
   water come up to? How do you know?
3) How many more lots of $\frac{1}{4}$ litre of water will we need to match the amount
   shown here?
4) Count in $\frac{1}{4}$ litres from zero up to the water level shown here.
   Write down your count.
5) Explain why you cannot count in $\frac{1}{2}$ litres from zero up to this water level.
6) Where could you start so it does work?

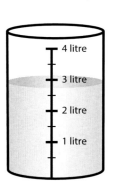

UNIT 15 · Recognising fractions of different amounts

National Curriculum link:

Recognise, find, name and write fractions $\frac{1}{3}$, $\frac{1}{4}$, $\frac{2}{4}$ and $\frac{3}{4}$ of a length, shape, set of objects or quantity.

Write simple fractions, for example $\frac{1}{2}$ of 6 = 3, and recognise the equivalence of $\frac{2}{4}$ and $\frac{1}{2}$.

Year 2 pupils should already know that:

- Unit fractions are connected to equal sharing
- Fractions are numbers and can be placed on the number line
- Two quarters are equivalent to a half

Supporting understanding

Throughout Year 2 we have used a range of pictures and resources to help children make sense of fractions.

Here, sticks of cubes are used as a talking point.

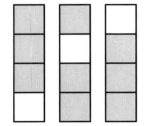

$\frac{1}{4}$ of each stick is white. Do you agree?

Recognising fractions of different amounts

The problem can then be developed to look at a quarter represented in a different way. Children should be encouraged to explain whether the previous statement '$\frac{1}{4}$ of each stick is white' is still true.

What would you expect children to say?

We should be careful not to represent fractions only as pictures where the number of equal parts shown is the same as the denominator. For example, we can show halves using pictures of two quarters or four eighths.

Pictures need to be varied so that children have to think about the fraction of the whole, as in the picture above.

ANSWERS
Task A: Table showing half of each total number of cubes
Challenge: 2
Task B: Table showing $\frac{1}{4}$ and $\frac{3}{4}$ of each total number of cubes
Challenge: 4
Task C: Table showing $\frac{1}{3}$ and number of cubes in the rest of the stick each time **Challenge:** They are the numbers when counting in threes from zero; they are in the 3-times table; they are multiples of three, etc. $\frac{1}{3}$ of 21 = 7

In the classroom

Ask children to use two different colours of cubes, e.g. blue and green, to make a stick that is $\frac{1}{2}$ blue.

What fraction can you use to describe the green part of the stick?

Use children's examples and count the parts as fractions to equal one whole. Look for children who have used, say, eight cubes and made four blue.

Show other sticks made with e.g. 4, 8 or 10 cubes in total.

What do we notice about the total number of cubes in each stick? (It is even.)

Use **Talking point** Picture 1.

Izzy has been making sticks of cubes as well.

She chose white and grey cubes.

Ask children to consider Izzy's question. Some groups could copy Izzy's sticks to help. Agree that each is $\frac{1}{4}$ white.

What do we know about the grey part each time? Why?

Izzy made another stick of cubes where $\frac{1}{4}$ is white.

Ask children to explore Izzy's thinking using Picture 2 and their own cubes.

Picture 3 can then be used to model the quarters.

Pose these, or similar, questions for different groups to consider:

- *What fraction of the stick is grey?*
- *Can you complete this number sentence: $\frac{1}{4}$ of ... = ... ?*
- *What do you notice about the total number of cubes in the stick each time? Do you think there is a pattern?*

Show a stick of three cubes with $\frac{1}{3}$ white.

Explain that we can show other fractions with cubes in the same way. Some groups will find out more about thirds in the tasks.

Talking point

Picture 1

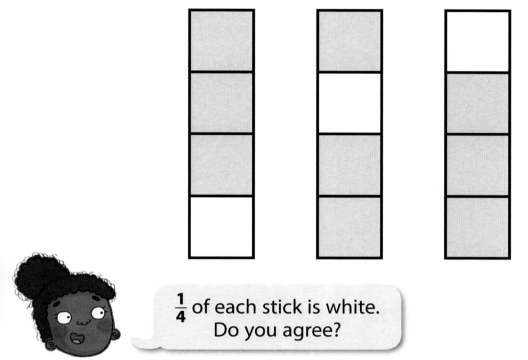

$\frac{1}{4}$ of each stick is white.
Do you agree?

Picture 2

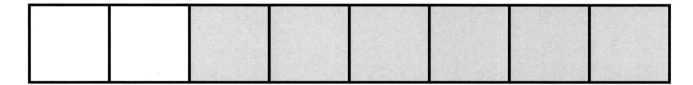

Picture 3

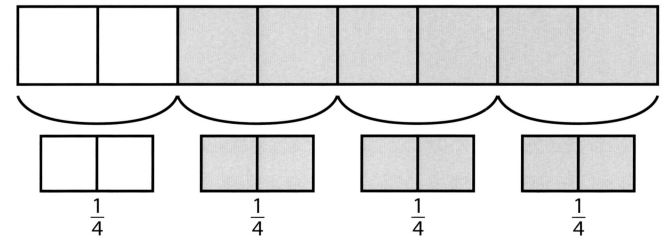

Unit 15: Recognising fractions of different amounts

Task A (Independent task)

Investigate making sticks that show $\frac{1}{2}$ each time.
Copy and complete this table to help you.

Challenge:
Use your stick of eight cubes, but show $\frac{1}{4}$ this time.
How many cubes are in your $\frac{1}{4}$?

Total number of cubes in the stick	2	4	6						
Number of cubes in $\frac{1}{2}$ of the stick	1								

Task B (Independent task)

Investigate making sticks that show $\frac{1}{4}$ each time.
Copy and complete this table to help you.

Total number of cubes in the stick	4	8				
Number of cubes in $\frac{1}{4}$ of the stick	1					
Number of cubes in $\frac{3}{4}$ of the stick	3					

Challenge:
I have 12 cubes in my stick. How many cubes are in $\frac{1}{3}$ of it?

Task C (Independent task)

Investigate making sticks that show $\frac{1}{3}$ each time.
Copy and complete this table to help you.

Total number of cubes in the stick	3	6				
Number of cubes in $\frac{1}{3}$ of the stick	1					
Number of cubes in the rest of the stick	2					

Challenge:
Look at the total number of cubes in the stick each time. Explain any patterns you see.
Use what you have found out to complete this: $\frac{1}{3}$ of ___ = 7.

Fluency with Fractions YEAR 2 © Rising Stars UK Ltd. 2014